Faces *of the* First People

NATIVE
AMERICAN
PORTRAITS
1865–1935

A BOOK OF POSTCARDS

PALACE OF THE GOVERNORS
PHOTO ARCHIVES, SANTA FE

Pomegranate
SAN FRANCISCO

Pomegranate Communications, Inc.
Box 808022, Petaluma CA 94975
800 227 1428; www.pomegranate.com

Pomegranate Europe Ltd.
Unit 1, Heathcote Business Centre, Hurlbutt Road
Warwick, Warwickshire CV34 6TD, UK
[+44] 0 1926 430111; sales@pomeurope.co.uk

ISBN 978-0-7649-6338-4
Pomegranate Catalog No. AA747

Pomegranate publishes books of postcards on a wide range of subjects.
Please contact the publisher for more information.

Cover designed by Patrice Morris
Printed in Korea
21 20 19 18 17 16 15 14 13 12   10 9 8 7 6 5 4 3 2 1

To facilitate detachment of the postcards from this book, fold each card along its perforation line before tearing.

The thirty images in this book of postcards were selected from the exhibition *Native American Portraits: Points of Inquiry,* presented by the New Mexico History Museum in Santa Fe. Drawing from the Palace of the Governors Photo Archives, the exhibit featured more than fifty historically significant Native American portraits that explore three distinct periods of time representing Native Americans in photographs.

The earliest photographs date from the late 1860s to about 1880. These images are examples of the government's systematic attempts to build a visual catalog representing Indian tribes. The prints reflect the relationship between Native Americans and government delegations. Many were produced by government exploration and economic initiatives, through private patronage, and as a result of western expansion. The goal was to document the wishful theory of the "vanishing" Indian while preserving material and scientific information.

The next group, 1880–1900, shows the focus on commercial photography and narrative photo-essays by regional professional and amateur photographers to promote development and tourism. It explores the growth of documentary/ethnographic photography. Portraiture of individuals was the bread and butter of this micro-economy and was often undertaken to boost the potential development of an area for industry and tourism.

The last period, 1900–1935, was driven by artistic notions of the Pictorial movement based on soft focus, richly textured papers, and dramatic dark prints in the style of Whistler and others that were painterly in intention. The photographs emphasize grand photographic issues of character to be found in the subject—strength, courage, wisdom, and beauty. Romantic symbolism and mythology of the vanishing Indian became ubiquitous through tourist publications by the railroad companies and the Fred Harvey Company, and by Edward Curtis in the grandest project of all, *The North American Indian,* funded by J. P. Morgan. When Pictorial photography fell out of fashion in the 1930s and the economy crashed, so did this style of portraiture, which was supplanted by hard-edged documentary photographic prints and modernist abstractions.

A collection of historic gems from the Palace of the Governors Photo Archives can be browsed and purchased at the online digitized collection:

www.palaceofthegovernors.org/photoarchives.html

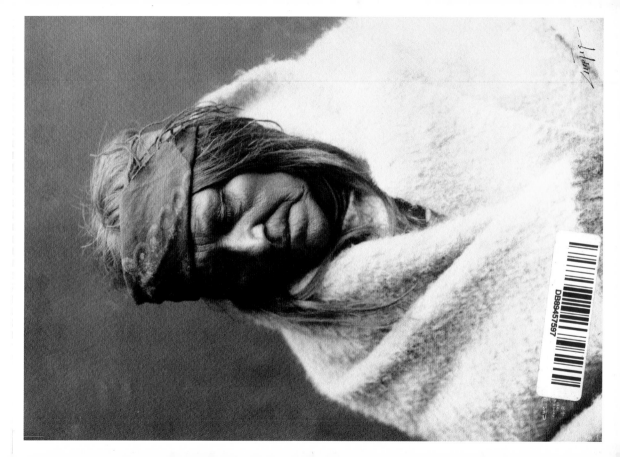

Faces *of the* First People

Edward S. Curtis (1868–1952)
Two Bear Woman, Piegan Blackfeet, Montana, 1900
Mercury toned platinum print, 16 x 11½ in.
Palace of the Governors Photo Archive Negative #103162

707 782 9000 WWW.POMEGRANATE.COM

Pomegranate

Faces *of the* First People

Jesse L. Nusbaum (1887–1975)
Woman and Baby, Jemez Pueblo, New Mexico, 1914
Toned gelatin silver print, 6 x 4¼ in.
Palace of the Governors Photo Archive Negative #61712

707 782 9000 WWW.POMEGRANATE.COM

Pomegranate

Faces *of the* First People

T. Harmon Parkhurst (1883–1952)
Patricio Calabaza, Santo Domingo Pueblo, New Mexico,
c. 1925–1930
Toned gelatin silver print, 7 x 5 in.
Palace of the Governors Photo Archive Negative #46763

707 782 9000   WWW.POMEGRANATE.COM

Pomegranate

Faces *of the* First People

Karl Moon (1878–1948)
Loti, Laguna Pueblo, New Mexico, 1907
Toned gelatin silver print, 14 x 10 in.
Palace of the Governors Photo Archive Negative #146660

Faces *of the* First People

De Lancey W. Gill (1859–1940)
Hoiio-Wotoma, Wolf Robe, Cheyenne, 1909
Hand-colored platinum print, 7¾ x 6 in.
Palace of the Governors Photo Archive Negative #86994

707 782 9000 WWW.POMEGRANATE.COM

Pomegranate

Faces *of the* First People

Antonio Zeno Shindler (1827–1880)
Moses Keokuk, Sauk and Fox, 1868
Albumen print, 10 x 8 in.
Palace of the Governors Photo Archive Negative #56181

WWW.POMEGRANATE.COM

707 782 9000

Pomegranate

Faces *of the* First People

T. Harmon Parkhurst (1883–1952)
Pueblo Girl, New Mexico, 1925–1930
Hand-colored gelatin silver print, 6¾ x 4¾ in.
Palace of the Governors Photo Archive Negative
#HP.2009.60.2

Faces *of the* First People

Unknown photographer
Two Native American Men, c. 1870–1880
Ninth-plate tintype, 3¼ x 2 in.
Palace of the Governors Photo Archive Negative #77737

707 782 9000   WWW.POMEGRANATE.COM

Pomegranate

Faces *of the* First People

Jeremiah Gurney & Son (1812–1886)
Bird Chief, Second War Chief of the Arapahos, 1871
Albumen print, 8 x 6 in.
Palace of the Governors Photo Archive Negative #58644

707 782 9000   WWW.POMEGRANATE.COM

Pomegranate

Faces *of the* First People

De Lancey W. Gill (1859–1940)
Mary L. Baldwin, Chippewa, 1914
Platinum print, 8½ x 6½ in.
Palace of the Governors Photo Archive Negative #59442

707 782 9000   WWW.POMEGRANATE.COM

Pomegranate

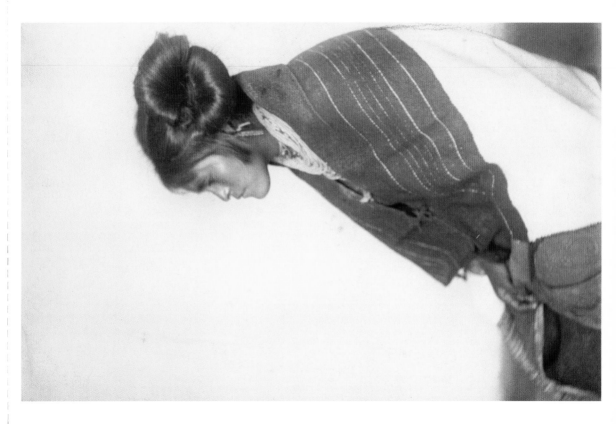

Faces *of the* First People

Carl Werntz (1874–1944)
Hopi Girl, Arizona, c. 1910–1920
Gelatin silver print, 6½ x 4 in.
Palace of the Governors Photo Archive Negative #37555

WWW.POMEGRANATE.COM

707 782 9000

Pomegranate

Faces *of the* First People

T. Harmon Parkhurst (1883–1952)
Pitacio Quintana, Santo Domingo Pueblo, New Mexico, 1916
Toned gelatin silver print, 19¾ x 16 in.
Palace of the Governors Photo Archive Negative #4309

Faces *of the* First People

Jeremiah Gurney & Son (1812–1886)
Tak-kee-o-mah, Little Robe, Chief of the Cheyennes, 1871
Albumen print, 8 x 6 in.
Palace of the Governors Photo Archive Negative #58646

WWW.POMEGRANATE.COM

707 782 9000

Pomegranate

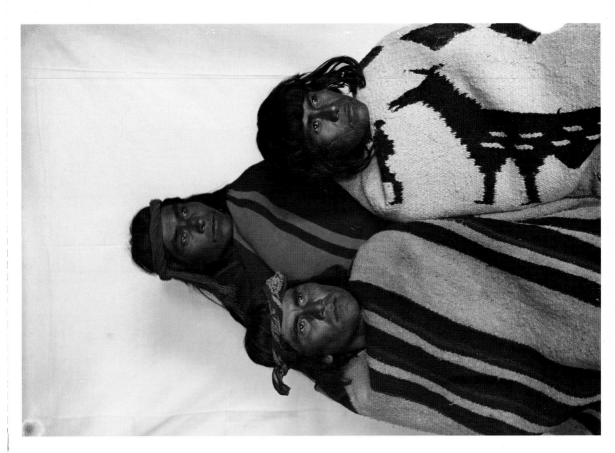

Faces *of the* First People

Unknown photographer
Three Pueblo Men, c. 1910–1915
Glass plate positive, 7 x 5 in.
Palace of the Governors Photo Archive Negative #81879

Faces *of the* First People

T. Harmon Parkhurst (1883–1952)
Caroline Trujillo, Cochiti Pueblo, New Mexico, c. 1925–1930
Gelatin silver print, 6¾ x 4¾ in.
Palace of the Governors Photo Archive Negative #2326

OSCAR OF THE LITTLE VESSEL. WASCO

Faces *of the* First People

Charles M. Bell (1848–1893)
Oscar or Little Vessel, Wasco, c. 1874
Albumen print, 6½ x 4¼ in.
Palace of the Governors Photo Archive Negative #87544

Faces *of the* First People

T. Harmon Parkhurst (1883–1952)
Pueblo Girl, New Mexico, 1925–1930
Hand-colored gelatin silver print, 14 x 10¾ in.
Palace of the Governors Photo Archive Negative #89802

707 782 9000   WWW.POMEGRANATE.COM

Pomegranate

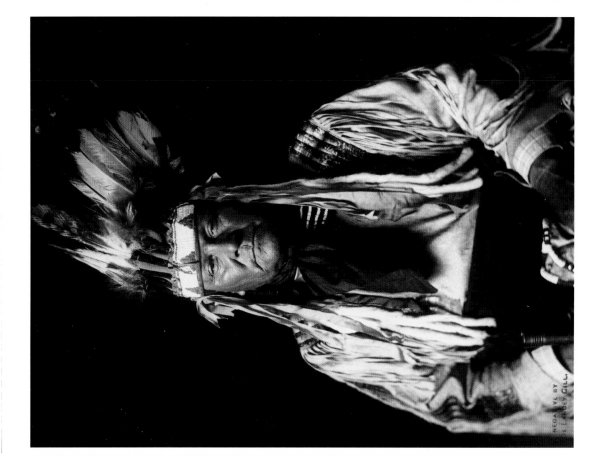

Faces *of the* First People

De Lancey W. Gill (1859–1940)
Baqugi, Big Boy also Arnold Woolworth, Arapaho, 1909
Platinum print, 8½ x 6½ in.
Palace of the Governors Photo Archive Negative #59445

707 782 9000   WWW.POMEGRANATE.COM

Pomegranate

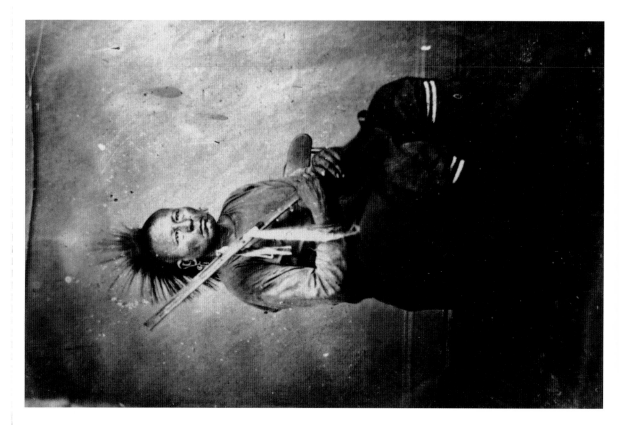

Faces *of the* First People

Antonio Zeno Shindler (1827–1880)
Wah-tian-kah, Osage, c. 1865–1868
Albumen print, 10 x 8 in.
Palace of the Governors Photo Archive Negative #56166

WWW.POMEGRANATE.COM

707 782 9000

Pomegranate

Faces *of the* First People

De Lancey W. Gill (1859–1940)
Wife of DK Lone Wolf, Kiowa, 1913
Hand-colored platinum print, 7¾ x 5½ in.
Palace of the Governors Photo Archive Negative #87001

707 782 9000   WWW.POMEGRANATE.COM

Pomegranate

Faces *of the* First People

Jesse L. Nusbaum (1887–1975)
Jemez Pueblo Man, New Mexico, 1914
Toned gelatin silver print, 6¾ x 4¾ in.
Palace of the Governors Photo Archive Negative #61706

707 782 9000   WWW.POMEGRANATE.COM

Pomegranate

Faces *of the* First People

Antonio Zeno Shindler (1827–1880)
Charles Keokuk, Sauk and Fox, 1868
Albumen print, 10 x 8 in.
Palace of the Governors Photo Archive Negative #56173

707 782 9000 WWW.POMEGRANATE.COM

Pomegranate

Faces *of the* First People

Charles M. Bell (1848–1893)
Manuelito, Navajo, c. 1874
Albumen print, 6½ x 4¼ in.
Palace of the Governors Photo Archive Negative #15949

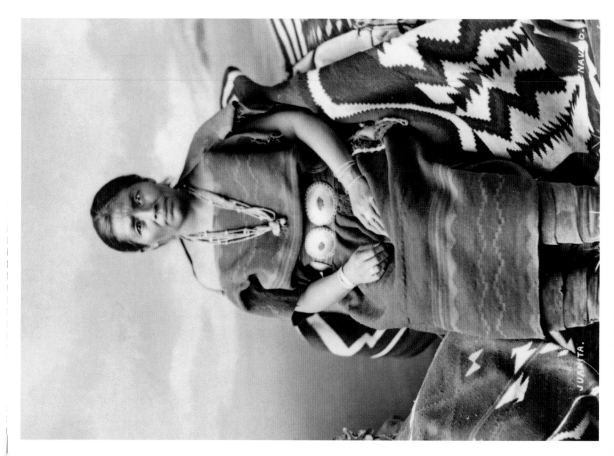

Faces *of the* First People

Charles M. Bell (1848–1893)
Juanita, Wife of Manuelito, Navajo, c. 1874
Albumen print, 6½ x 4¼ in.
Palace of the Governors Photo Archive Negative #59435

707 782 9000   WWW.POMEGRANATE.COM

Pomegranate

Faces *of the* First People

Jesse L. Nusbaum (1887–1975)
Santiago Naranjo, Santa Clara Pueblo, New Mexico, 1910
Toned gelatin silver print, 6¾ x 4¾ in.
Palace of the Governors Photo Archive Negative #61709

WWW.POMEGRANATE.COM

707 782 9000

Pomegranate

Faces *of the* First People

Charles M. Bell (1848–1893)
Tak-kee-o-mah, Little Robe, Chief of the Cheyennes, c. 1873
Albumen print, 11 x 8½ in.
Palace of the Governors Photo Archive Negative #58636

707 782 9000   WWW.POMEGRANATE.COM

Pomegranate

Faces *of the* First People

Charles M. Bell (1848–1893)
Semeo or Umatilla Jim, Warm Springs, c. 1874
Albumen print, 6½ x 4¼ in.
Palace of the Governors Photo Archive Negative #87543

Faces *of the* First People

G. Ben Wittick (1843–1903)
Navajo Man, One of Guilfoyle's Scouts in Apache War,
c. 1883–1886
Albumen print, 7 x 4 in.
Palace of the Governors Photo Archive Negative #15936

707 782 9000 WWW.POMEGRANATE.COM

Pomegranate

San Juan Chief of Mescalero Apaches

Wittick Photo

Faces *of the* First People

G. Ben Wittick (1843–1903)
San Juan, Chief of Mescalero Apache, 1883
Albumen print, 8½ x 5¼ in.
Palace of the Governors Photo Archive Negative #15893

WWW.POMEGRANATE.COM

707 782 9000

Pomegranate

Faces *of the* First People

G. Ben Wittick (1843–1903)
Mojave Woman, 1883
Albumen print, 8½ x 5¼ in.
Palace of the Governors Photo Archive Negative #15961

WWW.POMEGRANATE.COM

707 782 9000

Pomegranate